this or that?

moth

OR

butterfly?

Susan Kralovansky

Consulting Editor, Diane Craig, M.A./Reading Specialist

Super Sandcastle

An Imprint of Abdo Publishing
www.abdopublishing.com

visit us at www.abdopublishing.com

Published by Abdo Publishing, a division of ABDO, PO Box 398166, Minneapolis, Minnesota 55439. Copyright © 2015 by Abdo Consulting Group, Inc. International copyrights reserved in all countries. No part of this book may be reproduced in any form without written permission from the publisher. Super SandCastle™ is a trademark and logo of Abdo Publishing.

Printed in the United States of America, North Mankato, Minnesota
062014
092014

Editor: Liz Salzmann
Content Developer: Nancy Tuminelly
Cover and Interior Design and Production: Mighty Media, Inc.
Photo Credits: Kelly Doudna, Shutterstock

Library of Congress Cataloging-in-Publication Data
Kralovansky, Susan Holt, author.
  Moth or butterfly? / Susan Kralovansky ; consulting editor, Diane Craig, M.A., reading specialist.
     pages cm. -- (This or that?)
  Audience: 004-010.
  ISBN 978-1-62403-288-2
1. Moths--Juvenile literature. 2. Butterflies--Juvenile literature. I. Craig, Diane, editor. II. Title.
  QL544.2 *30116000836323*
  595.78--dc23
                       2013041831

Super SandCastle™ books are created by a team of professional educators, reading specialists, and content developers around five essential components—phonemic awareness, phonics, vocabulary, text comprehension, and fluency—to assist young readers as they develop reading skills and strategies and increase their general knowledge. All books are written, reviewed, and leveled for guided reading, early reading intervention, and Accelerated Reader® programs for use in shared, guided, and independent reading and writing activities to support a balanced approach to literacy instruction.

contents

moth or butterfly?

Is it a moth? Or a butterfly? Can you tell the difference?

Moths and butterflies both begin as eggs. Then they **hatch** as caterpillars.

A caterpillar creates a hard shell called a chrysalis. It turns into a moth or butterfly inside the chrysalis.

cocoon or not?

A moth caterpillar often wraps its chrysalis in silk. This makes an extra **layer** called a cocoon.

Most butterfly caterpillars do not make cocoons. The chrysalis is the only layer.

day or night?

Most butterflies are active during the day. When butterflies rest, they fold their wings.

Butterflies taste with their feet. **Female** butterflies taste plants to find good places to lay eggs.

Most moths are active at night. They hide during the day. Some moths rest with their wings open. Others rest with their wings folded.

wonderful wings

Moths and butterflies have scaly wings. The scales look like **shingles** on a roof.

Most moth wings are dull colors. Some moths look like wood or leaves. This helps them hide.

Most butterflies have colorful wings.

Some butterflies and moths have spots on their wings. The spots look like eyes. This can **confuse** predators.

thick or thin?

Moths have thick, furry bodies.

Butterflies have thinner bodies with less fur than moths.

fantastic feelers

Moths and butterflies have feelers on their heads. They are called antennae. Moth feelers are thick. They can look like feathers.

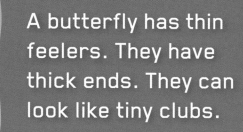

A butterfly has thin feelers. They have thick ends. They can look like tiny clubs.

at a glance

moth ———————— butterfly

starts as a caterpillar ———————— starts as a caterpillar

active at night ———————— active during the day

dull colored ———————— brightly colored

thick body ———————— thin body

antennae look feathery ———————— antennae have thick ends

moth finger puppet

go buggy! make a moth finger puppet.

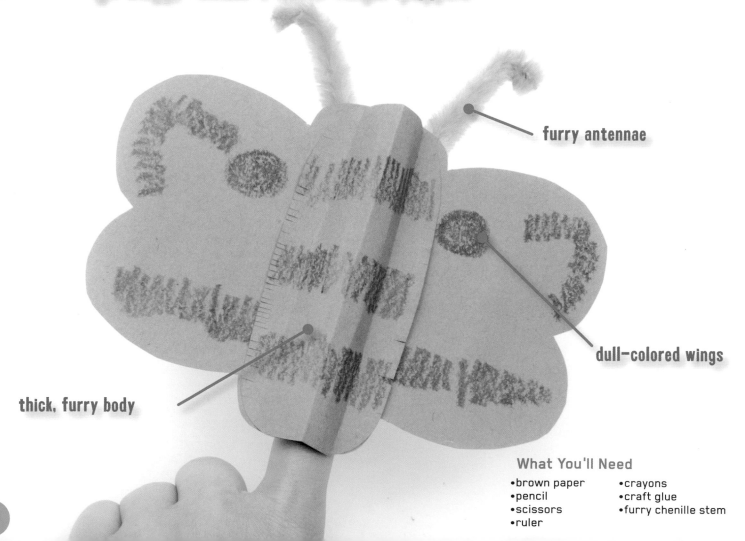

furry antennae

dull-colored wings

thick, furry body

What You'll Need
- brown paper
- pencil
- scissors
- ruler
- crayons
- craft glue
- furry chenille stem

1. Fold a piece of brown paper crosswise. Draw a moth wing along the fold. Include a bump at each end for the head and tail. Draw half of a thick moth body along the fold. Make it as long as the wing. Cut out the wing and body through both **layers** of paper.

2. Unfold the wings and body. Decorate them with crayons.

3. Fold the body in half again. Make short cuts along the unfolded edges.

4. Put glue behind the long edges of the body. Press the body over the fold of the wings. Let the glue dry.

5. Cut two 3-inch (7.5 cm) pieces of chenille stem. Curl one end of each piece. Glue the straight ends to the back of the moth. These are the antennae.

6. Cut a 3-inch (7.5 cm) by 1-inch (2.5 cm) piece of paper. Put glue on each short end. Glue it to the back of the moth. Leave enough space for your finger to fit under the strip. Let the glue dry.

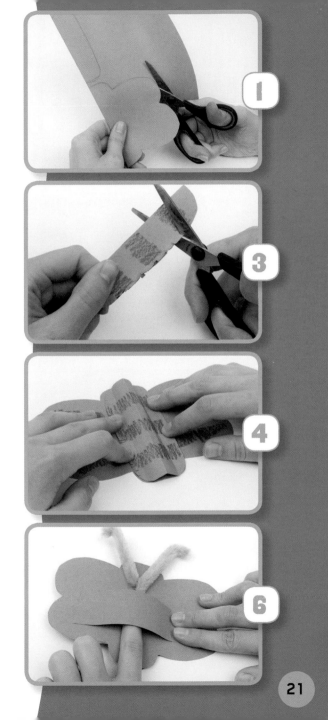

butterfly finger puppet

let your imagination fly with this butterfly finger puppet!

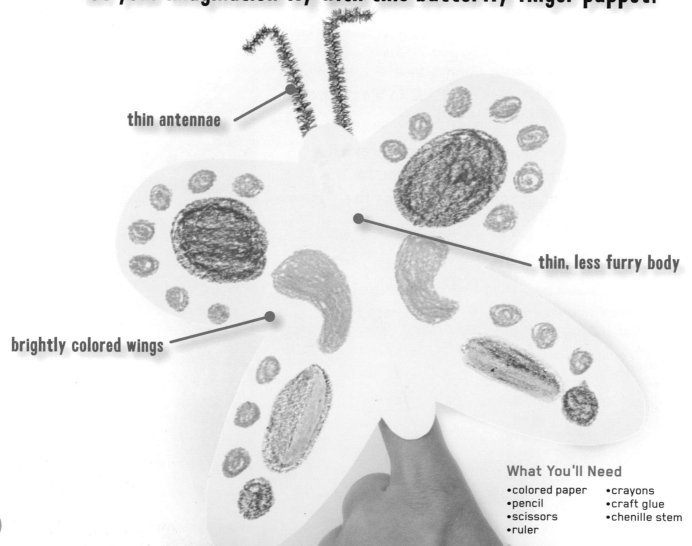

thin antennae

thin, less furry body

brightly colored wings

22

What You'll Need
- colored paper
- pencil
- scissors
- ruler
- crayons
- craft glue
- chenille stem

1. Fold a piece of colored paper in half crosswise. Draw a butterfly wing along the fold. Include a bump at each end for the head and tail. Cut out the wing through both **layers** of paper.

2. Unfold the wings. Decorate them with crayons.

3. Cut two 3-inch (7.5 cm) pieces of chenille stem. Bend one end of each piece. Glue the straight ends to the back of the butterfly. These are the antennae.

4. Cut a 3-inch (7.5 cm) by 1-inch (2.5 cm) piece of paper. Put glue on each short end. Glue it to the back of the butterfly. Leave enough space for your finger to fit under the strip. Let the glue dry.

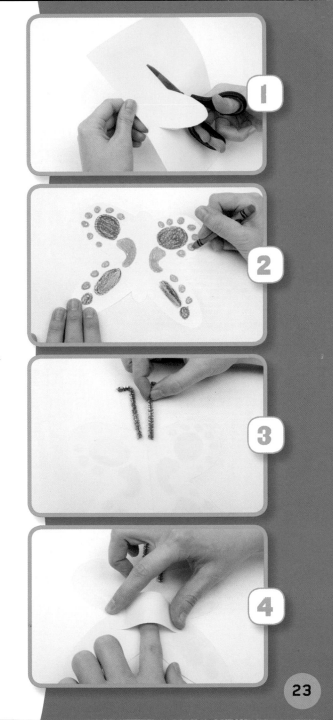

glossary

confuse – to make uncertain or unclear.

female – being of the sex that can produce eggs or give birth. Mothers are female.

hatch – to break out of an egg.

layer – one thickness of a material or a substance lying over or under another.

shingle – one of the thin tiles that go on the roof or sides of a building.